# Food for Crawlers

**Simple Strategies to Build Traffic to Your Website**

Jorge Armando Pérez

**Nüregime™ Graphics**
P.O. Box 211325
Chula Vista, CA 91921
(619)781-8134
Find us on the World Wide Web at: www.nuregime.com


To report errors, send a note to *errata@nuregime.com*


ISBN: 978-0-6152-1354-5


Printed in the U.S.A.

They say:

**"If you build it, they will come"**

I say:

**"Not so easy"**

# Table of Contents

# INTRODUCTION

There is no magic when it comes to the things you can do to get a good position in search engines, which translates into traffic to your website. In my experience, it boils down to two basic choices.

Choice #1: Spend thousands of dollars (some companies expend millions) in direct advertising such as paid banner placement, paid "top of the search engine page advertising," and announcing your website in more traditional media such as television, billboards, magazines, etc...

Choice #2: Optimizing your website the right way using all the specifics I number below, then submitting the site to search engines, directories, social networks, RSS-based content sites, etc., strategically using the methods and tools included in these pages. By the way, if you prefer to use Choice #1, you still have to optimize and submit the site, so Choice #2 is a must.

In this book I intend to show you Choice #2: an inexpensive, practical, and easy way to bring traffic to your website. Because you know your business (and your business needs) better than anyone else, it is important that you involve yourself in this process.

This guide is designed to be used in collaboration between "the client" and "the developer."

# CHAPTER 1

**OPTIMIZATION: First Things First.**

Note: Optimization is part of the construction of a good website. The optimization must be done prior to submitting your site to the search engines. At Nüregime™ we optimize all sites as part of our site building service.

You need to make sure your web developer has done all the steps listed below before you can be ready to take advantage of these technologies when submitting your site to the various places I will mention in the section on submitting.

**The Meta Tags**

The word meta stands for "situated behind or beyond." The meta tags contain a general description of the page, keywords, and copyright information. Search engines often display the contents of the Title tag and Distribution tag as the short summary you see on the results page. The Keywords tag also helps to place a page in the right results.

**Keywords and Target Phrases**

Keywords and target phrases must be relevant to the content and/or services the website offers. They should be strategically placed after studying what words are being used to find your competition.

The first thing we will need to do is determine the direction of campaign in relation to the key phrases we are choosing to target.

**Many site owners know immediately what phrases they want.**

If you feel like you know what you want, before you start, take a brief step back and assess if this really is the best phrase for your site. Yes, it just may very well be the perfect phrase, but if it isn't, you could wind up spending a lot of time and money pursuing a ranking that either will never happen or will provide very little value for your site.

**What to look at when choosing a target phrase.**

1. Relevance—Is this phrase relevant to your site and its content?

2. Search frequency—Are people even searching for this phrase?

3. Competition—How competitive is this field? Is it even a feasible target?

# Choosing the Right Words and Phrases

**Create a List of Phrases**

Before looking up search frequencies and competition, you need to create a list of relevant phrases. Open up an Excel spreadsheet and type out all relevant phrases that come to mind. Do a little brainstorming, as there are no wrong answers at this state.

After you have exhausted your thoughts, go to your website. Navigate throughout it, recording any keyword phrase ideas that spring up, checking your title tags and body content. Once this is done, do the same thing with your competition. Visit some sites that you know are in direct competition with you and go through them, recording any relevant phrases you see.

By now, you should have a long list of potential targets, a list that will grow further as you look into their search frequencies.

**It is O.K. to Use a Keyword Tool**

There are several keyword tools to choose from, two of the more popular being WordTracker® and Keyword Discovery(© Trellian), although many still use the free Overture® tool. It is important to note that no keyword tools give you 100% accurate search figures. In most cases, you will get numbers representing a sampling from various search engines. These numbers are best used in comparing one phrase to another to find out which is more popular rather than determining specifically how much traffic to expect.

## Keyword Tools and Search Frequency

Once you've opened up a keyword tool, begin entering your keyword phrases and record their noted search frequency. Be sure to scroll through the results, recording any additional phrases that are both relevant and have acceptable search frequencies. The exact number of searches required to make a phrase acceptable depends widely on industry and even on the search tool being used. A phrase with only 100 searches per month may be perfect for a secondary target, but in most cases it may not be the best bet for a primary phrase.

## Sorting Your List

You now should have a very exhaustive list of potential target phrases and their corresponding search frequencies. Sort this list in descending order based on the number of searches so that the most popular phrase is at the very top. In many industries, the top few phrases may be completely impractical to target due to the competition, but we'll determine that a bit later.

## Check the Competition

The next step is to get a feel for how competitive these phrases are. In the next column in your spreadsheet, place the number of results returned by Google™ for each individual phrase. The lower the number of competing pages, in most cases, the easier it may be to achieve rankings. Note: this is not always the case, but it is an indicator.

At this point, you will have a long list sorted by search frequency, along with the number of competing pages. If you are fortunate, you will see one phrase immediately that jumps out—solid searches with low competition. This just may be the most ideal target phrase.

Does this phrase fit well with the theme of your site? If so, go to Google™ and take a closer look at the ranking websites. Does your site fit in with the general feel of these results? In some cases it may not, as your phrase could have different meanings (especially true if using acronyms). This phrase may represent a completely different part of the world if geographically targeted, or simply may be littered with mega competitors such as eBay®, Amazon™, Wikipedia, and others. If you can see your site fitting in with these results, it's time to assess the general feasibility of this phrase.

Take a look at the number of back links and indexed pages that each site has. Do your numbers compare? If you find that the top 10 ranking sites all have back links well into the tens of thousands, and your site has a dozen or so, you may want to consider a different phrase. If the ranking sites are in the high tens, or low hundreds, and your site has a dozen links, then you have something to work with if you are willing to work on increasing your link counts. The number of pages indexed is less important than links, but if you have a 6-page site and you are planning on competing with thousand-page sites, your chances of success will be much lower.

The real key is to try to find a phrase that offers relevance, decent searches, and competition that is not way out of your league.

## How to Drive Qualified Traffic

For organic SEO, it is usually best to focus on one primary phrase that best suits your site, while also targeting more specific secondary phrases for relevant sections of your site. With organic SEO, the number of phrases you should target is somewhat limited by the size of your site. The larger the site, the more phrases you will have the ability to work towards.

The phrase with the most searches is not always the best fit. This is largely true with the real estate market.

For example:

Let's say I use the Overture Keyword Selector Tool for an example. The phrase "real estate" saw 3,057,037 searches in January of 2008. On the surface, this phrase seems like a dream come true, but you have to consider the geographic issues.

If your office serves the San Diego area, is someone searching in New York likely to be a qualified visitor to your site? In most cases, no. Targeting the phrase "San Diego real estate," with 12,441 searches, seems like a much better choice as it would deliver more qualified traffic. While this phrase is still quite competitive, it is not nearly as difficult as simply "real estate." Take a look at the big picture and determine not only how likely it is that you may achieve rankings, but whether the traffic generated from such a ranking would actually have a positive impact on sales.

## The Title Tag

The Title tag plays one of the most important roles in search results at Google™ and is almost always the heading Google™ chooses for each of its listings. Placement of your target phrase is best used near the start of the tag and repeated again in the middle or near the end. Three uses of your target phrase may be helpful in some instances, as long as it is not too overwhelming. For best results, each page on your site should have a totally unique title tag.

It is also important to remember that because Google™ will use this title as the main heading for your listings, you will want to keep it attractive to potential searchers. Also, try to add a call to action or other wording to help make your listing appear attractive to searchers.

To help illustrate the fact Google™ takes this tag into consideration, simply do a search for your target phrase and take a look at the titles of the top 10. I tried a search for a rather broad term, "design," and saw that 8 out of 10 listings had it in the title tag, and 2 out of 10 had it as the very first word.

If you do only one thing to your website, make sure that all your title tags are relevant, unique, and contain your target phrase for each page.

I have configured some of the big content sites I have built to show the title of each page article as a title in the meta tags. That way, each page in the sitemap will present a title relevant to content to the search engines, especially Google.™

**The Description Tag**

The Description tag is still occasionally used by Google™ as the description that appears in the search results themselves. While this used to be a more common practice, Google™ tends to use it most often on sites with very limited content or those which are Flash-based. It is still being used for content rich sites, but this is less common.

The Description tag still has an impact on search rankings. Your best bet when using this tag is to keep it short and sweet with your target phrase close to the start and not repeated more than 3 times. Like the Title tag, each page on your site should have its own unique description tag.

# CHAPTER 2

**Other Uses of Words**

**Keywords in Domain**

There is still some question about whether having a target phrase as part of your top level domain (TLD) is of use to search rankings. From my experience, yes, there is value here, although, nothing like it used to be some years ago.

If you are starting off in the online world and are contemplating which domain to go for, consider one that uses your target phrase, assuming that it is both relevant to your business name and uses no more than a single hyphen. While multiple hyphens in a domain can be successful, they are very common with highly spammy websites, so it is best to not take that route if possible.

While having a keyword as part of your domain can provide some ranking substance, I would not suggest heading out and doing a domain swap. In most cases, you would be better off working on your existing site than starting from scratch with a new domain.

**Keywords in Page-Specific URLs**

Using keywords for specific page URLs can also help add a little bit of value to your site, provided you use them responsibly. Consider using a keyword as a directory name and as part of a file name where it naturally makes sense to do so.

Example.
If I want to promote the web design side of my site, I can use
nuregime.com/web/design

**Link Anchor Text**

This is the actual text you click on as part of a link. When full or partial target phrases are used within your text links, they help pass on some value to the linked page for those phrases. This is also true when considering surrounding text. When the content around the link is also relevant, the link holds slightly more value.

While a link that simply states "click here" or "www.example.com" does have its place, they provide considerably less value than a link that uses "web design" as its anchor.

## Image Alt Text

While image alt text still plays a minor role, its biggest part is in image-based navigation. If you have an image linked to another page, the alt text will be attributed much the same way as standard link anchor text is.

Image alt text should always be short and to the point, and it should accurately describe either the image itself or the page the image is linking to. Do not use Alt tags as a place to stuff keywords.

## Inline Links

These are links that are found mid-sentence or mid-paragraph as opposed to a simple listing of links as found in a menu or possibly on a sitemap. Links found mid-paragraph tend to pass on a little more value from the surrounding text and can provide more relevance to the linked page.

## Site Navigation

It is absolutely imperative that your website be fully spiderable by the search engines. This may seem obvious, but often webmasters overlook Google's ability to crawl a website. Google™ has become very advanced in what links it can follow and how it can spider a website, but there are still some things that can cause significant roadblocks.

Flash:
One of the most commonly made mistakes is the use of Flash. If Flash is used as the sole means of site navigation, then you can count on Google™ not viewing your internal pages and having a significant disadvantage in terms of site rankings.

Java Script/DHTML:

These days, most Java Script and even DHTML menus can be spidered by Google,™ but, this is not always the case. If your site utilizes any kind of fancy navigation and you are wondering why Google™ has not indexed your internal pages, check out Google's cached text version of your page. If you do not see any text links, then your navigation may be invisible to Google.™

Images:

Image-based navigation has been safe for many years now, but if your site uses this form of navigation, it is essential to have brief, relevant alt text on all your buttons. This alt text will act much like standard anchor text for text-based links. This is not just for the purpose of search ranking value. Take a look at Google's cached text version of your page. If you have image-based links that do not have alt text, those links do not appear. This doesn't mean Google™ won't follow them, but for anyone viewing your site on a text-based browser, your links will be invisible to them.

# CHAPTER 3

**Real Food for the Crawlers.**

Simple definition of crawlers: also known as a "robot" or "spider," a crawler is an automated software program that runs at many search engines, reads sites' content, analyzes it, and inserts them into the index (or collects information for later insertion into the index).

Now that we have the right keywords, phrases, and other words selected, in position, and functioning correctly, we can start getting the site ready for the crawlers.

## 1. The robots.txt File

The robots.txt file is a set of instructions for visiting robots (spiders) that index the content of your website's pages. For those spiders that obey the file, it provides a map for what they can and cannot index.

## 2. Search Engine-Friendly Links

One of the most fundamental steps in SEO is to make your links "crawlable." Developers that use a lot of PHP scripts in websites are forced to go back and make all links "engine-friendly." PHP places characters in the links such as [?=&], and the search engines' spiders cannot read these links.

Most search engines use robots to crawl sites and then classify the content and keywords into a database. Google™ even keeps an archived copy of the site in case it goes down or if the page is pulled off, which is a very useful way to access information that has stopped being available. By having non-crawlable links, robots won't get very far on your site, minimizing the pages that will end up in the search engine's index.

## 3. RSS Feeds

RSS feeds are a fairly a new format of XML that is intended to share information in a condensed form (such as a title, description, and link to a new article). They are good for syndication. Many current browsers have native support for RSS feeds, but older browsers will display RSS pages as XML code.

There are more and more networks where you can send your feeds and in turn bring readers to your content. Also, visitors to your site can subscribe to your feeds and read them using a reader (many e-mail clients now support RSS reading) or even add your feeds to their home page as content such as My Yahoo! and others. Read more about RSS in Chapter 5.

## 4. The Sitemap

A sitemap is not only a page listing the structure of your pages, although that's a sitemap in itself. In optimization language, sitemaps are an easy way to inform search engines about pages on sites that are available for crawling. In its simplest form, a sitemap is an XML file that lists URLs for a site along with additional metadata about each URL (when it was last updated, how often it changes, and how important it is relative to other URLs in the site) so that search engines can more intelligently crawl the site.

Web crawlers usually discover pages from links within the site and from other sites. Sitemaps supplement this data to allow crawlers that support sitemaps to pick up all URLs in the sitemap and learn about those URLs using the associated metadata.

# CHAPTER 4

**SUBMISSION**

**Note:** *If a site is not optimized, don't bother to submit it anywhere. You'll be wasting your time.*

Now that all the mechanism is in place, we are ready to have fun. Let the world know what you have built!

**What is Search Engine Submission?**

Search engine submission is the process of notifying search engines of the existence of website content so that they include the site in their indexes and search results. Most major search sites frequently revisit already indexed sites to ensure that their search results reflect current content.

**The process in 2 stages.**

1. We (the developer) send your site to all major search engines initially.

2. You (the client) continue to send the site to directories, social networks, RSS content-based sites, etc., following the guide we include in the next chapter.

In detail:

**I. We send the site to all major engines.**

At Nüregime™ we use advanced tools to send your site to engines and networks. After we send the site, we create reports tracking all the results even weeks later.

1. Errors for URLs in sitemaps

2. HTTP errors

3. Broken links and not found pages

4. URLs restricted by robots.txt

5. Diagnostics to see errors and problems encountered by crawlers while accessing pages on your site

6. Content analysis to see potential problems with site metadata, such as title and meta description information

7. Top search queries to see which search queries most often returned pages from your site, and which of them were clicked

8. Crawl stats to see your distribution info for your site, including the current page rank for pages on your site

9. Subscriber stats. If your site publishes feeds of its content, this page will display the number of users who have subscribed to these feeds using Google™ products such as iGoogle,™ Google Reader,™ or Orkut.™

10. What Googlebot™ sees to find details about how the Googlebot™ sees your site

11. Index stats to learn how your site is indexed by Google,™ including which pages are indexed and which other sites point to your site

12. Sitemap reports, number of pages, updated submissions

13. Set geographic target and associate a particular geographic location with this site if you are targeting users within that area

14. Enhanced image search, which enables Google's enhanced search for images on your site, including advanced labeling techniques for images hosted by Google™

**II. We also send your RSS xml pages and blogs to several networks simultaneously.**

More details on blogs, RSS, and social networks in the next chapter.

For a complete list of search engines, go to our SEO page:

nuregime.com/seo

# CHAPTER 5

**Blogs, RSS, and Social Networks**

Now that your site is optimized and submitted to search engines, you can do some additional things that will help you create traffic.

**Blogs**

Simple definition of blog: A blog (short for weblog) is a personal online journal that is frequently updated and intended for general public consumption. Blogs are defined by their format: a series of entries posted to a single page in reverse-chronological order.

**What does a blog has to do with traffic?**

A blog has content. You can write anything related to your business and any information or articles for your clients or visitors.

The good thing is that your blog content can be syndicated, people can subscribe to your blog content via RSS, and again, your content can be sent to different networks... More on this later.

**Preparing Your Blog to Interlink with Social Networks.**

We have integrated a mechanism to some of our clients' blogs to make it easy for users to bookmark the blog using their preferred social network.

1. With a tool called "Social Tags," you are going to tag it from your site to all the big social networks and back.

2. Open accounts in all the blog networks in the list I provide on our site, and then link entries you have in your blog. THIS IS REALLY IMPORTANT.

For a complete list of social network sites, go to our SEO page: nuregime.com/seo

**RSS Feeds**

RSS is a family of web feed formats used to publish frequently updated digital content, such as blogs, news feeds, or podcasts.

As more and more people get involved with the Internet and as more websites, blogs, news services, and other online resources continue to grow in number and variety, it becomes increasingly important to maintain high visibility and exposure for the content being generated by closely following the major distribution media.

Until recently, the use of major search engines and directories has been the main vehicle for reaching websites and other HTML-based content pages.

As a rapidly increasing number of content sources, new and old, migrate or add RSS as a key distribution channel and as more people utilize RSS newsreaders and aggregators to keep themselves informed, the ability to maintain high exposure and visibility is gradually shifting from a complete attention to major search engines and content optimization techniques to an increasing awareness of RSS feed directories and search tools.

I have included in our site's SEO section a long (and frequently updated) list of places where you can and should submit your RSS feeds.

One of the key benefits of this list is that it provides all of the submission links directly so that you don't have to waste any time at all to find these at each destination site. This by itself is a significant effort, especially as a number of sites make it purposely hard to find this information in order to discourage spam and superficial or automated submissions.

I think this is a very useful list to increase your RSS feed/blog exposure and visibility online.

**Tip:** I recommend you create an Excel spreadsheet to track your process through it. You can do the whole effort in less than a day, and you can start to see the results the day after.

To access the list, go to:

nuregime.com/seo

---

and select the "Submit RSS Feeds" option. I have also included a list of RSS readers.

**Reading the RSS Feeds**

An aggregator or news aggregator or feed reader is client software that uses a web feed to retrieve syndicated web content such as weblogs, podcasts, vlogs, and mainstream mass media websites, or in the case of a search aggregator, a customized set of search results.

Aggregators reduce the time and effort needed to regularly check websites for updates, creating a unique information space or "personal newspaper." Once subscribed to a feed, an aggregator is able to check for new content at user-determined intervals and retrieve the update.

The content is sometimes described as being "pulled" to the subscriber, as opposed to "pushed" via email or IM. Unlike recipients of some "pushed" information, the aggregator user can easily unsubscribe from a feed.

Aggregator features are frequently built into portal sites (such as My Yahoo! and iGoogle™), modern web browsers, and email programs.

**Web-based Aggregators**

Web-based aggregators are applications that reside on remote servers and are typically available as web applications such as Google Reader™ or Bloglines. Because the application is available via the web, it can be accessed anywhere by a user with an Internet connection.

Since RSS is so powerful for distributing content and in return getting traffic back to your site, it is important that you take the time to submit RSS content everywhere possible.

# CHAPTER 6

**Local Directories and Mirror Pages**

**Local Directories**

Most of the major search engines permit you to list your website and attach it to a specific geographic area. These locally-focused websites include Google Local, Yahoo Local, MSN Local, InfoUSA, Merchant Circle, TrueLocal.com, Local.com, CraigsList.com, and others.

Often local media, organizations, or businesses offer locally-based directories where you can list your business for free. Places you might check in your local area include regional or local newspapers, television stations, regional or city magazines, independently owned local directories, city guides of major search engines (like Yahoo City Guide), profession or industry directories, regional/state sites, and chamber of commerce or visitor bureau sites.

**Tip:** Ask your local clients where they look online for local goods and services to give you an idea of the sites your target market actually uses.

## See Where Your Competition Is

A good way to find new directories is to go to a search engine and search to see where your competition is. Make sure you have a presence in each of those directories.

When you become a member of local directories, you are going to have the opportunity to enter a description of your business. It's a good idea to include words and phrases that relate to your content.

If a business directory has a blog, take advantage of it and remember to mention your site's URL or domain name, and link everything back to your site at every opportunity you get. Google™ reads all those links, and that improves your ranking.

You can also go to our site, where we have a list of local directories and resources:

nuregime.com/seo

## Mirror Pages

Create mirrors of the front page of the site or a simple one-page site directed to your home page. Take advantage of free communities like Geocities. To do this, you can ask your designer to make a simple index.htm page (containing all meta tags) and upload that file to every free service you can find out there.

If they don't allow you to upload HTML files, then just create a simple page using a color that matches your site, and place a link to your site.

Remember, every time you create a mirror page; submit it to all the search engines you can find.

For a complete list of places where you can create and/or upload your mirror pages and a list of search engines where you can submit your created mirror pages, go to our SEO page:

nuregime.com/seo

**More Good Ideas**

1. When you create a mirror page, use your domain name as the username, as this becomes part of the URL in most cases.

2. Once you get your static URL for each blog or social Site, submit that URL to all the search engines.

3. Remember to write down your login information because you will need to go back every once in a while and upload or post new entries.

4. It's a good idea to dedicate an e-mail account just for this because once you start opening accounts in social networks, you'll get a lot more mail than usual, along with people commenting on your entries.

# CHAPTER 7

**Track Your Progress**

In this final chapter, I would like to mention some easy-to-use and practical tools to help you see the results of your hard work.

I know that as you have been putting into practice all the advice I've been giving you here, it has taken a great deal of work and dedication, and it is only fair that you start seeing some of the results of your hard work right away.

Remember that this is a process and that to achieve a real strong presence on the web takes time. Most of the submissions to search engines take 3 or 4 weeks to show in the search results, but some of the submissions to local directories, RSS feeds, and other media I mentioned in previous chapters will start to return good results much sooner than that.

Now, how can you see the progress you've made without some good tools to track it?

Here are some good tools.

By the way, you don't have to be a web developer or have server access to be able to use most of these tools.

# Google Analytics

Google Analytics can help you learn even more about where your visitors come from and how they interact with your site and strengthen your marketing initiatives, creating higher-converting websites.

With this tool, you can see how many people have visited to your site and how extensively they interacted with your content. This traffic overview allows you to drill down and view the characteristics of different visitor segments and examine the different factors that make up visit quality (i.e. average page views, time on site, and bounce rate).

**Tip:** When you sign up for this service, the program is going to ask you to insert a piece of JavaScript in all the pages you want the crawler to read and report. You need to ask your website developer to insert that code for you.

In the case of large sites with databases and PHP mechanisms, the JavaScript will need to be entered on the index.php or an includer.

**Conversions**

This tool will also help you see how many visitors are being converted into clients or prospects by tracking the actions they take on the site such as downloading a file or a presentation, signing up for a product tour, becoming members of the site, or signing up for the mailing list.

## Setting Goals

You can set goals and work towards the completion of those goals.

The Google Analytics Funnel Visualization report (in the Goals section) will help you identify where you are losing visitors on the path to conversion. The center column shows the conversion path that you expect visitors to take. The right-hand column shows where the visitors who leave the funnel go. The left-hand column shows where the visitors who enter the funnel come from.

Use this report to identify steps where visitors lose interest. Go back and tighten up these critical pages. Make sure the next steps are always clear and that you aren't asking for too much from your visitors.

To summarize, you'll maximize return from the visitors you attract if you do the following things:

1.  Create key activities (goals) on your site.

2.  Get that first click towards conversion.

3.  Call your audience to action on each page.

4.  Simplify the conversion path.

5.  Experiment and measure!

# adCenter Labs

MSN has re-launched its entire search marketing tools into one area called AdCenter Labs.

It's a great tool for search marketers and anyone looking to gain some insight into the world of keyword marketing and the progression of how people search using an engine.

The data comes primarily from MSN's own engine, but it's clear that this data would apply across any search engine.

Some features been added to the new system are:

- Hierarchical Keyword Suggestion
- Enter a keyword and display semantically related words that are organized hierarchically.
- Keyword Price Estimation

# Yahoo Site Explorer

**Site Explorer** allows you to explore all the web pages indexed by Yahoo! Search. View the most popular pages from any site, dive into a comprehensive sitemap, and find pages that link to that site or any page.

Again, just like Google Analytics™ or any other tool, you will need to authenticate your site. In this case, instead of adding a piece of code, you will just upload a file to the root directory of your website. If don't have FTP access to your server, just ask your web developer to add the file for you. The reason for authenticating your site is obvious: additional data about your site and functionality is subject to abuse if made available to someone who does not own or manage the site so Yahoo! will not share additional data about a site until the authentication process is successfully completed.

With this tool, you can see all the pages that the Yahoo! search engine has in its database. If you see that Yahoo! is missing any of your pages, you can resubmit that specific page. Like any other search engine, Yahoo! makes no guarantees about when or whether your URL will appear as a search result, so again, I recommend submitting everything anyway. In my experience, most of the time I see really good results.

**More Tools**

There many other good tools to help you track your traffic and submission results.
Go to our website for a whole section on SEO tools:

nuregime.com/seo

**Final Words**

The web is an ever-changing world. Most tools evolve, and new technologies are born. It is a constantly moving environment.

We keep an eye on everything that can help our clients achieve their individual goals.

I believe that:

**"In helping others to reach their dreams, I grow"**

## About the Author

Jorge is the founder of Nüregime™ Graphics, a web development and graphic design company based in San Diego, California. He has an Applied Sciences in Graphic Design degree and has transitioned to new media, becoming an influential voice in the field, especially in the area of CSS, xHTML, and Web 2.0 standards-based websites construction. Everything he builds is based upon two principles, creativity and simplicity. Whether it's web development, print, branding, identity processes, or any other kind of innovation, his passion for design is evident in his work.

## In the words of others...

Seldom have I had the good fortune to find someone as responsive and capable as Jorge of Nüregime™ is. He quickly transitioned my vague website ideas to eye-catching appeal with real dynamics. Jorge brought the essence of my books to a few colorful and easy-to-follow pages. He knows what he is doing!

*—Dr. Ernest Blase, Author of Hostage Moscow*

In most cases, if you find a technical inclined person, he or she lacks in creativity, and when you find a creative person, he or she does not have an understanding of the technical aspect of the media, in this case the web space. Jorge has both; he is a consummate artist that is excellent in the understanding of the technical space.

*—Hector Melendez, GM, LLP*

# Glossary

Frequently used terms in this book:

Accessibility—Refers to a web page or website that people interacting with different kinds of disabilities and the difficulty they can experience due to physical and or technological barriers. A web page or site that addresses these users' limitations is said to be accessible.

Bandwidth—Bandwidth is the amount of data that can be transferred over the network in a fixed amount of time. On the Internet, it is usually expressed in bits per second (bps). A hosting server will allocate your site a fixed amount of bandwidth usage within a regular period of time.

Blog—Short for web log, a blog is a web page that serves as a publicly accessible personal journal for an individual. Typically updated daily, blogs often reflect the personality of the author.

Browser—Often called a web browser, it is simply a software application used to interpret HTML commands and display page content. The two most popular browsers are Microsoft Internet Explorer (IE) and Netscape Navigator.

Content—A word you'll likely see a lot is "web content" and by definition, content is the 'stuff' that makes up a web site. This could be words, pictures, images, or sounds. In essence, however, when we talk about web content, we are essentially referring to content of a textual nature. Content, therefore, is the 'information' in text form that a website provides.

CSS [Cascading Style Sheets]—A simple mechanism for adding style (i.e., fonts, colors, spacing) to web documents. Not all browsers (or specific versions) implement the full specifications for CSS.

Directory—A database edited manually by humans. Sites are indexed by category, making this feature the main difference from a search engine. Users can navigate through the categories to locate documents or information. Most directories offer searching options (which are similar to searching using a search engine) within its database.

DNS [Domain Name System (Service)]—An Internet system/service that translates domain names into IP addresses. Domain names are alphabetic so they're easier to remember. The Internet, however, is really based on IP addresses. Every time you use a domain name, therefore, a DNS service must translate the name into the corresponding IP address.

Domain Name—A unique name that identifies one or more IP addresses. Domain names are used in URLs to identify particular websites. Every website is located by its unique IP address.

Hits—The individual requests a server answers in order to render a single webpage completely. The page document itself and the various images on the page represent a separate hit.

Home Page—The first page (also referred to as an opening page, start page, or main page) of a website. This would technically be your index page or default page of your directory.

Hosting—Usually refers to a computer (or a network of servers) that stores the files of a website that has web server software running on it, connected to the Internet. Your site is then said to be hosted.

HTML [Hypertext Markup Language]—HTML is a basic markup language derived from the Standardized General Markup Language (SGML), providing the means for creating simple hypertext documents intended for publishing on the World Wide Web.

Internet—A global network connecting millions of computers. Each Internet computer, called a host, is independent. The Internet is not synonymous with the World Wide Web. The Internet and the web are two related but separate things.

IP [Internet Protocol]—The method or protocol by which data is sent from one computer to another on the Internet. Each computer (known as a host) on the Internet has at least one IP address that uniquely distinguishes it from all other computers on the Internet.

JavaScript—JavaScript is an object-based, client-side scripting language developed by Netscape. Embedded in the head section of a web document, it can produce interactivity to a web page dynamically.

Keywords—A word used by a search engine in its search for relevant web pages.

Link [Hyperlink]—An element in an electronic document that links to another place in the same document or to an entirely different document. Typically, you click on the hyperlink to follow the link. Hyperlinks are the most essential ingredient of all hypertext systems, including the World Wide Web.

Meta Tags—The word meta stands for "situated behind or beyond." The meta tags contain a general description of the page, keywords and copyright information. Search engines often display the Title tag and Distribution meta tag as the short summary you see on the results page.

Optimization—Search engine optimization (SEO) is the process of improving the volume and quality of traffic to a website from search engines via "natural" ("organic" or "algorithmic") search results for targeted keywords. Usually, the earlier a site is presented in the search results or the higher it "ranks," the more searchers will visit that site. SEO can also target different kinds of searches, including image searches, local searches, and industry-specific vertical search engines.

As a marketing strategy for increasing a site's relevance, SEO considers how search algorithms work and what people search for. SEO efforts may involve a site's coding, presentation, and structure, as well as fixing problems that could prevent search engine indexing programs from fully spidering a site. Other, more noticeable efforts may include adding unique content to a site, ensuring that content is easily indexed by search engine robots, and making the site more appealing to users.

Organic SEO—Organic Search Engine Optimization is the SEM term for unpaid, high-ranking results on search engines.

PHP [Hypertext Preprocessor]—A server-side, HTML embedded scripting language used to create dynamic web pages. Designed for Windows and UNIX type platforms.

Ranking—The number (order of ranking; i.e., 1 being the highest) that a website is listed for a specific search term in a specific search engine. Search engines utilize a ranking algorithm (mathematical formulas, variables, and set of weights) to determine a site's ranking for a particular keyword or keyword phrase.

Resolution—The resolution of an image describes how fine the dots are that make up that image. The more dots, the higher the resolution. When displayed on a monitor, the dots are called pixels. A 640 x 480 screen (resolution) is capable of displaying 640 distinct dots on each of its 480 lines, or about 300,000 pixels.

RSS—The acronym used to describe the de facto standard for the syndication of web content. RSS is an XML-based format and while it can be used in different ways for content distribution, its most widespread usage is in distributing news headlines on the web. A website that wants to allow other sites to publish some of its content creates an RSS document and registers the document with an RSS publisher. A user that can read RSS-distributed content can use the content on a different site. Syndicated content can include data such as news feeds, events listings, news stories, headlines, project updates, and excerpts from discussion forums or even corporate information.

Script—A script is an executable list of commands created by a scripting language. Scripts that are executed on a web server (i.e.; Perl, PHP) are said to be server-side scripts. Scripts that execute on your own home PC (i.e.; JavaScript) are said to be client-side scripts. Scripts can be embedded within HTML to produce a web page with dynamic actions.

Scripting Language—A scripting language is a simple programming language used to write an executable list of commands, called a script. JavaScript, Perl, VBscript are scripting languages rather than general-purpose programming languages.

Search Engine—A server (computer) or commonly a collection of servers dedicated to indexing Internet web pages, storing the results in a giant database and returning lists of pages that match particular searched queries from within its database. The indexes are normally and automatically generated using spiders.

Spider—An automated software robot that continuously crawls hyperlinks and pages on the Internet and collects data that is returned to its database for indexing. This is how search engines function. The process of crawling the web, storing URLs, and indexing keywords, links, and text is the act of spidering.

Server—A computer, program, or process that responds to requests for information from a user. On the Internet, all web pages reside on servers (computers).

Sub-Domain (Name)—A sub-domain is a domain that is part of a larger domain name. DNS hierarchy consists of the root-level domain at the top, underneath which are the top-level domains, followed by second-level domains and finally sub-domains.

Tag—An HTML tag is a formatting command written into a document that specifies how it should be formatted. A web browser interprets these tags and outputs the intended command (action).

Traffic—Similar to a real-world sense of traffic on a road or freeway, traffic in a web sense is a measurement of the number of users that visit a website.

URI [Uniform Resource Identifier]—The generic term for all types of names and addresses that refer to objects on the World Wide Web. A URL is one kind of URI.

URL [Uniform Resource Locator]—Each separate page accessible on the web has a unique address that can be identified by its URL. The first part of the address (i.e. http or ftp) indicates what protocol to use, and the second part specifies the IP address or the domain name where the resource is located.

Usability—Refers to the level or degree of a page's operating friendliness for the user.

Validation—Validation is a way to make sure that (HTML) code is compliant with current HTML specifications.

W3C [World Wide Web Consortium]—Established in October 1994 to lead the World Wide Web to its full potential by developing common protocols that promote its evolution and ensure its interoperability.

WWW [World Wide Web]—A way of accessing information over the medium of the Internet. Browsers such as Internet Explorer or Netscape are utilized to access the vast collection of interconnected (hyperlinked) documents on the web.

Contact us at:

**Nüregime™ Graphics**
P.O. Box 211325
Chula Vista, CA 91921
(619)781-8134
www.nuregime.com